Parenting with Purpose:
Character Development Through Faith

Parenting with Purpose:

Character Development Through Faith

Biblical Principles

Authored By:

Diana Gadus, M.Ed.

Parenting with Purpose
Raising Children with Character
Biblical Principles

Copyright 2024 by Diana Gadus, M.Ed.
Published by: Diana Gadus Inc.

All rights reserved. No part of this publication can be reproduced, stored in a retrievable system, or transmitted, in any form or by any means electronic, mechanical, photocopying, recording or otherwise except by the inclusion of brief quotations in a printed review, without prior written permission from the Publisher.

Diana Gadus, Inc
8711 Wesleyan Dr
Fort Myers, Fl 33919

THE HOLY BIBLE, NEW INTERNATIONAL VERSION®, NIV® Copyright © 1973, 1978, 1984, 2011 by Biblica, Inc.® Used by permission. All rights reserved worldwide.

Parenting with Purpose:
Character Development Through Faith

Copyright © 2024 by Diana Gadus, M.Ed.

All rights reserved. No portion of this book may be reproduced in any form without written permission from the publisher or author, except as permitted by U.S. copyright law.

This publication is designed to provide accurate and authoritative information in regard to the subject matter covered. It is sold with the understanding that neither the author nor the publisher is engaged in rendering legal, investment, accounting or other professional services. While the publisher and author have used their best efforts in preparing this book, they make no representations or warranties with respect to the accuracy or completeness of the contents of this book and specifically disclaim any implied warranties of merchantability or fitness for a particular purpose. No warranty may be created or extended by sales representatives or written sales materials. The advice and strategies contained herein may not be suitable for your situation. You should consult with a professional when appropriate. Neither the publisher nor the author shall be liable for any loss of profit or any other commercial damages, including but not limited to special, incidental, consequential, personal, or other damages.

Preface

My name is Diana Gadus and I have birthed and raised six children. This book came into being as an internal prompting to stay true to biblical principles that I tried to foster and instill in my children. I have been raising children since 1984. I have lived through the beginning of computers, the internet, cell phones, video games and social media. I am an educator and have begun my legacy of creating and establishing my real estate business. I have earned a Bachelor of Science in Business, Master of Education in School Counseling and Educational Leadership. I am a lifelong learner. I went to a Catholic High School and a Catholic University for Educational Leadership. I worked in Catholic Education for 8 years and the rest of my years in public education. I have seen societal and educational policy changes. Through all of the changes, I have always tried to instill a sense of God, prayer and biblical principles within my family and children. I felt very compelled to write this book with the idea of giving thought and ideas to parents for instilling character and biblical principles as guiding ideas in parenthood. By no means have I been the perfect parent, the best I can hope for is that my children continue to connect with God and their own life purpose.

Parenting with Purpose:
Character Development Through Faith

Introduction

Parenting is a journey, a path that winds through valleys of challenges and ascends mountains of triumphs. It is a sacred duty, a calling imbued with both joy and responsibility. As a mother of six, each child uniquely crafted by God, I have navigated this path with a heart full of love and a spirit anchored in faith. This book is a testament to the lessons learned, the wisdom gleaned, and the grace experienced through the years of raising my children from infancy to young adulthood, guided by the timeless principles of the Bible.

The Bible serves as our roadmap, offering divine insights and practical guidance for nurturing our children. Proverbs 22:6 (NIV) instructs us to "start children off on the way they should go, and even when they are old they will not turn from it." This verse encapsulates the essence of biblical parenting: to lay a foundation of faith and values that will sustain our children throughout their lives. But how do we practically apply these ancient truths to the modern complexities of parenting? This book seeks to answer that question.

Parenting with Purpose: Character Development Through Faith

Raising six children—each with their own personalities, strengths, and challenges—has taught me that there is no one-size-fits-all approach to parenting. My eldest daughter, born on April 6, 1984, is a beacon of creative thought and compassion, while my son, born on May 6, 1995, embodies analytical thinking and resilience. Each of my children has a distinct learning style and emotional sensitivity, requiring tailored approaches to their upbringing. This diversity within a single family highlights the importance of understanding and nurturing the individuality of each child.

This book is structured to guide you through various aspects of parenting, with each chapter delving into a specific area, supported by biblical references, real-life examples, and practical advice. We will explore the foundational principles of biblical parenting, emphasizing the importance of instilling faith and values from an early age. We will also discuss the role of discipline, drawing from scriptures such as Hebrews 12:11 (NIV): "No discipline seems pleasant at the time, but painful. Later on, however, it produces a harvest of righteousness and peace for those who have been trained by it."

Parenting with Purpose: Character Development Through Faith

Understanding the unique design of each child is crucial. Psalm 139:13-14 (NIV) reminds us that "you created my inmost being; you knit me together in my mother's womb. I praise you because I am fearfully and wonderfully made." Recognizing and celebrating the individuality of each child allows us to tailor our parenting approaches to meet their specific needs, fostering their growth and development.

Nurturing spiritual growth, encouraging educational success, and responding to emotional sensitivities are all integral parts of parenting. We will delve into these areas, providing strategies for creating a supportive and nurturing environment that promotes holistic development. Communication is key, and we will explore ways to foster open and honest dialogues with our children, ensuring they feel heard and valued.

Parenting with Purpose:
Character Development Through Faith

As children transition into adolescence and eventually into adulthood, our roles as parents evolve. Guiding them with wisdom, preparing them for independence, and instilling responsibility are essential tasks. We will discuss practical ways to support our children during these critical stages, ensuring they are equipped to navigate the challenges of life with faith and confidence.

Prayer is a powerful tool in parenting, and we will explore the significance of interceding for our children, trusting in God's plans for their lives. Sibling relationships, often marked by both camaraderie and conflict, will be examined, with strategies for fostering unity and love within the family.

Parental self-care is vital, as maintaining our well-being enables us to be effective caregivers. We will discuss the importance of balance, self-reflection, and reliance on God's strength. Ultimately, our goal is to leave a legacy of faith, character, and love, impacting not only our children but future generations.

Parenting with Purpose:
Character Development Through Faith

This book is a heartfelt journey through the seasons of parenting, offering insights and encouragement for those committed to raising their children with purpose and faith. As you embark on this journey, may you find inspiration and guidance in the timeless wisdom of the Bible, and may your efforts bear fruit in the lives of your children and beyond.

Chapter 1

Foundations of Biblical Parenting

Parenting with Purpose: Character Development Through Faith

The foundation of biblical parenting is built upon the understanding that children are a gift from God, entrusted to us to nurture, guide, and love. Psalm 127:3 (NIV) states, "Children are a heritage from the Lord, offspring a reward from him." This perspective transforms our approach to parenting, imbuing it with a sense of reverence and responsibility. As stewards of these precious lives, we are called to raise them in accordance with God's principles, ensuring they grow into individuals who reflect His love and truth.

The Bible provides a wealth of wisdom on parenting, offering both general principles and specific guidelines. At the core of biblical parenting is the concept of love—unconditional, selfless, and sacrificial. 1 Corinthians 13:4-7 (NIV) beautifully describes this love: "Love is patient, love is kind. It does not envy, it does not boast, it is not proud. It does not dishonor others, it is not self-seeking, it is not easily angered, it keeps no record of wrongs. Love does not delight in evil but rejoices with the truth. It always protects, always trusts, always hopes, always perseveres."

Parenting with Purpose:
Character Development Through Faith

Creating a Faith-Centered Home

A faith-centered home is one where God's presence is felt, His principles are taught, and His love is evident. Joshua 24:15 (NIV) declares, "But as for me and my household, we will serve the Lord." Creating such an environment involves intentional practices, such as regular family devotions, prayer, and worship. It also means integrating faith into everyday life, demonstrating how biblical principles apply to various situations and decisions.

The Importance of Modeling

Children learn not only through instruction but also through observation. Deuteronomy 6:6-7 (NIV) emphasizes the importance of modeling godly behavior: "These commandments that I give you today are to be on your hearts. Impress them on your children. Talk about them when you sit at home and when you walk along the road, when you lie down and when you get up." Our actions, attitudes, and responses to life's challenges provide a living example for our children. By embodying the values we wish to impart, we create a powerful and lasting impact.

Parenting with Purpose:
Character Development Through Faith

Establishing Boundaries and Expectations

Boundaries and expectations are essential components of effective parenting. Proverbs 29:17 (NIV) advises, "Discipline your children, and they will give you peace; they will bring you the delights you desire." Establishing clear rules and consistent consequences helps children understand the importance of accountability and responsibility. It is important, however, to balance discipline with grace, ensuring that our approach reflects God's loving nature.

The Role of Communication

Effective communication is foundational to a healthy parent-child relationship. James 1:19 (NIV) instructs, "Everyone should be quick to listen, slow to speak and slow to become angry." Active listening, empathetic responses, and open dialogues foster trust and understanding. It is through communication that we can guide, correct, and encourage our children, helping them navigate the complexities of life.

Conclusion

The foundations of biblical parenting are rooted in love, modeling, faith, boundaries, and communication. By adhering to these principles, we create a nurturing environment where our children can thrive. As we embark on this journey, let us remember the wisdom of Proverbs 22:6 (NIV): "Start children off on the way they should go, and even when they are old they will not turn from it." Our commitment to raising our children according to God's design will yield a legacy of faith and character that endures through generations.

Chapter 2

Understanding Individuality Unique Design of Each Individual

Parenting with Purpose: Character Development Through Faith

Every child is a masterpiece, uniquely crafted by the hand of God. Psalm 139:13-14 (NIV) beautifully captures this truth: "For you created my inmost being; you knit me together in my mother's womb. I praise you because I am fearfully and wonderfully made; your works are wonderful, I know that full well." Understanding and celebrating the individuality of each child is crucial to effective parenting. Each child has a distinct personality, learning style, and emotional makeup, requiring personalized approaches to their upbringing.

Recognizing Individual Strengths and Weaknesses

As parents, we must keenly observe and identify the unique strengths and weaknesses of each child. Some may excel academically, while others shine in creative arts or sports. Recognizing these differences helps us tailor our support and encouragement. Romans 12:6 (NIV) reminds us, "We have different gifts, according to the grace given to each of us." Embracing this diversity within our children allows us to nurture their God-given talents and guide them towards their true potential.

Parenting with Purpose:
Character Development Through Faith

Adapting Parenting Styles

One of the key challenges in parenting multiple children is adapting our parenting style to suit each child's needs. What works for one child may not necessarily be effective for another. My eldest daughter, with her artistic flair and sensitivity, required a nurturing and supportive approach, while my son, analytical and determined, responded better to clear expectations and logical reasoning. Proverbs 22:6 (NIV) advises, "Start children off on the way they should go, and even when they are old they will not turn from it." This verse underscores the importance of understanding each child's path and guiding them accordingly.

The Role of Temperament

Temperament plays a significant role in shaping a child's behavior and interactions. Some children are naturally more extroverted, while others are introverted. Recognizing these temperamental traits helps us create environments where our children feel comfortable and confident. 1 Peter 4:10 (NIV) encourages us to "use whatever gift you have received to serve others, as faithful stewards of God's grace in its various forms." By understanding and honoring our children's temperaments, we can help them develop their strengths and manage their challenges.

Parenting with Purpose:
Character Development Through Faith

Learning Styles and Educational Approaches

Children have diverse learning styles—visual, auditory, kinesthetic, and more. Understanding how each child learns best is essential for their educational success. My daughter, born on February 26, 1997, thrived with visual aids and hands-on activities, while my son, born on May 6, 1995, preferred reading and structured lessons. Proverbs 4:7 (NIV) states, "The beginning of wisdom is this: Get wisdom. Though it cost all you have, get understanding." Gaining insight into our children's learning preferences enables us to support their academic journey effectively.

Emotional Sensitivity and Support

Emotional sensitivity varies among children, requiring us to be attuned to their emotional needs and responses. Some children may be more resilient, while others may need extra reassurance and comfort. Ephesians 4:2 (NIV) advises, "Be completely humble and gentle; be patient, bearing with one another in love." Demonstrating empathy and understanding helps us build strong emotional connections with our children, fostering a sense of security and trust.

*Parenting with Purpose:
Character Development Through Faith*

Practical Strategies for Nurturing Individuality

Personalized Attention: Spend one-on-one time with each child, engaging in activities that interest them and encourage their passions. This individual attention shows them that they are valued and understood.

Encouragement and Affirmation: Regularly affirm your children's unique qualities and achievements. Positive reinforcement builds their confidence and self-esteem.

Flexibility in Parenting: Be willing to adjust your parenting methods to meet the needs of each child. Flexibility demonstrates your commitment to their well-being and growth.

Emotional Check-ins: Regularly check in with your children to understand their feelings and concerns. Open communication helps them express themselves and seek support when needed.

Educational Support: Collaborate with teachers and educators to create learning environments that cater to your children's strengths. Advocate for teaching methods that align with their learning styles.

Celebrating Differences: Foster an environment where differences are celebrated, and each child's uniqueness is honored. Encourage siblings to appreciate and support one another's strengths.

Conclusion

Understanding the individuality of each child is a cornerstone of effective parenting. By recognizing and nurturing their unique strengths, adapting our parenting styles, and providing tailored support, we can help our children thrive. Ephesians 2:10 (NIV) reminds us, "For we are God's handiwork, created in Christ Jesus to do good works, which God prepared in advance for us to do." As we embrace our children's individuality, we honor God's design and prepare them to fulfill their purpose.

Chapter 3

Nurturing Spiritual Growth in Children

Parenting with Purpose:
Character Development Through Faith

Spiritual growth is the foundation upon which all other aspects of a child's development are built. As parents, it is our privilege and responsibility to nurture our children's faith, guiding them to develop a personal relationship with God. Proverbs 22:6 (NIV) exhorts us, "Start children off on the way they should go, and even when they are old they will not turn from it." By embedding spiritual principles in their lives from an early age, we lay a solid foundation for their future.

The Importance of Spiritual Foundation

A strong spiritual foundation provides children with a moral compass and a sense of purpose. It shapes their values, influences their decisions, and equips them to face life's challenges with faith and resilience. Deuteronomy 6:6-7 (NIV) emphasizes the importance of teaching God's commandments to our children: "These commandments that I give you today are to be on your hearts. Impress them on your children. Talk about them when you sit at home and when you walk along the road, when you lie down and when you get up."

Parenting with Purpose:
Character Development Through Faith

Creating a Spiritually Rich Environment

Creating a spiritually rich environment at home involves intentional practices that foster faith and devotion. Here are some strategies to cultivate a God-centered atmosphere:

Daily Devotions: Establish a routine of daily devotions, including Bible reading, prayer, and worship. This practice helps children develop the habit of seeking God regularly. Chad Warner made some videos which are now digital called Veggie Tales. Listening to kids songs or bible kids songs in the car while running errands or traveling.

Scripture Memorization: Encourage children to memorize Bible verses. Psalm 119:11 (NIV) says, "I have hidden your word in my heart that I might not sin against you." Memorizing scripture equips children with spiritual truths that they can draw upon in times of need. This works for some kids. Children's church groups make a game of it and offer incentives.

Parenting with Purpose:
Character Development Through Faith

Faith Conversations: Integrate faith into everyday conversations. Discuss biblical principles and how they apply to various situations, helping children see the relevance of their faith in daily life.

Church Involvement: Regular attendance at church and participation in church activities provide children with a sense of community and opportunities to grow in their faith alongside others.

Role Modeling: Demonstrate a vibrant faith in your own life. Children learn by observing, so let them see you praying, reading the Bible, and living out your faith authentically. Reflect on your own actions and behaviors to understand the influence on your children.

Encouraging Prayer and Worship

Prayer and worship are vital components of a child's spiritual life. Teaching children to pray fosters a personal connection with God and instills the habit of seeking His guidance and comfort. Philippians 4:6 (NIV) encourages us, "Do not be anxious about anything, but in every situation, by prayer and petition, with thanksgiving, present your requests to God." Encourage children to pray about their worries, joys, and needs, helping them develop a trusting relationship with God. Pretend God is an invisible friend.

Worship, both individually and corporately, allows children to express their love and adoration for God. Create opportunities for worship at home through music, singing, and creative expressions like drawing or writing. Psalm 95:1-2 (NIV) invites us, "Come, let us sing for joy to the Lord; let us shout aloud to the Rock of our salvation. Let us come before him with thanksgiving and extol him with music and song."

*Parenting with Purpose:
Character Development Through Faith*

Instilling Biblical Values

Biblical values such as love, kindness, honesty, and integrity are essential for character development. Ephesians 4:32 (NIV) instructs us, "Be kind and compassionate to one another, forgiving each other, just as in Christ God forgave you." By teaching and modeling these values, we help our children develop a strong moral foundation.

Love and Compassion: Encourage acts of kindness and compassion towards others. Galatians 5:22-23 (NIV) lists the fruit of the Spirit, including love, joy, peace, patience, kindness, goodness, faithfulness, gentleness, and self-control. Foster these qualities in your children through service projects, helping others, and practicing empathy.

Parenting with Purpose: Character Development Through Faith

Love is the cornerstone of Christian values, encapsulating the essence of God's commandments. The Bible teaches us to love unconditionally and sacrificially, mirroring the love God has for us. "Above all, love each other deeply, because love covers over a multitude of sins." (1 Peter 4:8, NIV) This verse highlights the profound impact of love, emphasizing its power to heal and forgive. By loving deeply, we reflect God's love and create a foundation of compassion and understanding.

Compassion involves empathizing with others and taking action to alleviate their suffering. It reflects God's love and mercy. "Finally, all of you, be like-minded, be sympathetic, love one another, be compassionate and humble." (1 Peter 3:8, NIV) Compassion is a call to action. By showing empathy and kindness, we mirror God's love and care for humanity.

Parenting with Purpose: Character Development Through Faith

Honesty emphasize being truthful in words and actions in daily life. Proverbs 12:22 (NIV) states, "The Lord detests lying lips, but he delights in people who are trustworthy." Encourage children to be truthful and to act with integrity in all circumstances. Honesty involves being truthful and transparent in all dealings. It is a cornerstone of integrity and trust. "Therefore each of you must put off falsehood and speak truthfully to your neighbor, for we are all members of one body." (Ephesians 4:25, NIV) Honesty fosters trust and unity. By speaking truthfully, we build strong, authentic relationships and reflect God's truthfulness.

Integrity is a character trait grown from honesty and always doing the right thing in given situations. Integrity includes doing the right thing when nobody is looking. "The integrity of the upright guides them, but the unfaithful are destroyed by their duplicity." (Proverbs 11:3, NIV) This verse highlights the value of integrity and its role in guiding one's actions and decisions. It contrasts the steady, reliable path of those who live with integrity against the downfall of those who engage in deceit and dishonesty.

Parenting with Purpose:
Character Development Through Faith

In the book of Proverbs, wisdom literature, integrity is frequently emphasized as a hallmark of a righteous and godly life. It serves as a moral compass, helping individuals navigate life's challenges with honesty and uprightness. Integrity involves being truthful, consistent, and morally sound, even when no one is watching.

Imagine you're a middle school student, and during a math test, you notice that your best friend is trying to look at your answers. They're struggling and really need a good grade. It would be easy to let them copy, but practicing integrity means doing what's right, even when it's hard. So, you quietly cover your paper and after the test, you have a conversation with your friend. You explain why cheating isn't the right way to go, and you offer to help them study for the next test instead.

By acting with integrity, you're not only being honest but also helping your friend understand the importance of doing their own work. This builds trust and respect between you and your friend, and it sets a positive example for others. Plus, you'll feel good knowing that you did the right thing, and you'll gain a sense of inner peace and confidence.

Parenting with Purpose:
Character Development Through Faith

Practicing Integrity

Practicing integrity is crucial because it aligns our actions with our values and faith. It helps build trust, guides our decisions, enhances our reputation, and brings inner peace. By living a life of integrity, we reflect the character of Christ, who exemplified the highest standards of honesty and righteousness. Proverbs 11:3 reminds us that integrity is our guide, keeping us on the path of righteousness and away from the pitfalls of deceit. So, let's strive to practice integrity in all areas of our lives, knowing that it's a key component of a life well-lived and pleasing to God.

Remember, integrity isn't just about the big decisions; it's about the little choices we make every day. Whether you're a kid in school or an adult at work, practicing integrity means being honest, fair, and true to your values, no matter what.

Parenting with Purpose:
Character Development Through Faith

Teach the power of forgiveness. Matthew 6:14-15 (NIV) reminds us, "For if you forgive other people when they sin against you, your heavenly Father will also forgive you. But if you do not forgive others their sins, your Father will not forgive your sins." Help children understand the importance of letting go of grudges and extending grace to others. Forgiveness is the act of pardoning others as God has pardoned us through Christ. It is essential for maintaining healthy relationships and spiritual well-being. "Be kind and compassionate to one another, forgiving each other, just as in Christ God forgave you." (Ephesians 4:32, NIV) This verse calls believers to forgive as they have been forgiven. It promotes healing and reconciliation, reflecting God's grace and mercy.

Faith is the assurance of things hoped for and the conviction of things not seen. It is the bedrock of a relationship with God, trusting in His promises and His plan. "Now faith is confidence in what we hope for and assurance about what we do not see." (Hebrews 11:1, NIV) Faith requires trusting in God's unseen plans and believing in His promises. It encourages reliance on God's wisdom and timing, fostering spiritual growth and resilience.

Parenting with Purpose:
Character Development Through Faith

Joy in the Christian context is a deep-seated sense of happiness that comes from a relationship with God. It transcends circumstances, rooted in the assurance of God's love and salvation. "Rejoice in the Lord always. I will say it again: Rejoice!" (Philippians 4:4, NIV) This verse encourages believers to find joy in their relationship with the Lord. It teaches that true joy is not dependent on external situations but on the inner assurance of God's presence and love.

Self-control is the ability to regulate one's emotions, thoughts, and behavior in the face of temptations and impulses. It is essential for maintaining a righteous and godly life. "For the Spirit God gave us does not make us timid, but gives us power, love and self-discipline." (2 Timothy 1:7, NIV) This verse underscores the importance of self-discipline as a fruit of the Spirit. It empowers believers to live disciplined lives, guided by God's love and strength.

Parenting with Purpose:
Character Development Through Faith

Gentleness is a quality of being kind, tender, and mild-mannered. It reflects a Christ-like attitude in dealing with others, promoting peace and understanding. "Let your gentleness be evident to all. The Lord is near." (Philippians 4:5, NIV) Gentleness is a testament to God's presence in our lives. By being gentle, we show the world the compassionate and caring nature of Christ.

Humility involves recognizing our dependence on God and valuing others above ourselves. It is the antidote to pride and fosters a spirit of service and cooperation. "Humble yourselves before the Lord, and he will lift you up." (James 4:10, NIV) Humility invites God's favor and elevation. By humbling ourselves, we acknowledge God's sovereignty and our need for His guidance.

Obedience to God is a fundamental aspect of Christian faith, demonstrating trust and submission to His will. "If you love me, keep my commands." (John 14:15, NIV) Obedience is a sign of love for God. By keeping His commandments, we show our commitment to His teachings and our desire to live according to His will.

Parenting with Purpose:
Character Development Through Faith

Patience is the capacity to accept or tolerate delay, trouble, or suffering without getting angry or upset. It is a virtue that reflects trust in God's timing. "Be completely humble and gentle; be patient, bearing with one another in love." (Ephesians 4:2, NIV) Patience involves enduring hardships and delays with a calm spirit, trusting in God's timing and purpose. It promotes harmony and understanding in relationships.

Generosity is the willingness to give freely and abundantly, reflecting God's grace and provision. "Each of you should give what you have decided in your heart to give, not reluctantly or under compulsion, for God loves a cheerful giver." (2 Corinthians 9:7, NIV) Generosity flows from a heart transformed by God's love. It involves giving joyfully and selflessly, trusting that God will provide for all our needs.

Service to others is a fundamental Christian duty, reflecting Jesus' example of selfless love and compassion. "For even the Son of Man did not come to be served, but to serve, and to give his life as a ransom for many." (Mark 10:45, NIV) Jesus' life exemplified service. By serving others, we follow His example and demonstrate God's love in action.

Parenting with Purpose:
Character Development Through Faith

Responsibility involves taking ownership of one's actions and obligations. It is a sign of maturity and reliability. "Whatever you do, work at it with all your heart, as working for the Lord, not for human masters." (Colossians 3:23, NIV) This verse encourages diligent and responsible behavior, reminding us that our actions are ultimately accountable to God.

Perseverance involves steadfastness in the face of difficulties, relying on God's strength to overcome challenges. "Let us not become weary in doing good, for at the proper time we will reap a harvest if we do not give up." (Galatians 6:9, NIV) Perseverance is crucial for achieving God's purposes. By remaining steadfast, we trust in God's timing and His promise of reward.

Peacefulness involves maintaining tranquility and harmony, even in challenging circumstances. It reflects God's peace in our hearts. "Blessed are the peacemakers, for they will be called children of God." (Matthew 5:9, NIV) Peacemakers reflect God's kingdom on earth. By fostering peace, we demonstrate God's transformative power in our lives.

Parenting with Purpose:
Character Development Through Faith

Spiritual Milestones and Celebrations

Celebrating spiritual milestones reinforces the significance of faith in a child's life. Baptisms, first communions, and other significant events provide opportunities for families to come together and celebrate God's work in their children's lives. Psalm 78:4 (NIV) urges us, "We will not hide them from their descendants; we will tell the next generation the praiseworthy deeds of the Lord, his power, and the wonders he has done." Use these occasions to share stories of God's faithfulness and to encourage continued spiritual growth.

Conclusion

Parenting with Purpose: Character Development Through Faith

Nurturing spiritual growth in children is a profound and rewarding aspect of parenting. By creating a spiritually rich environment, encouraging prayer and worship, instilling biblical values, and celebrating spiritual milestones, we lay a foundation of faith that will sustain our children throughout their lives. As Proverbs 22:6 (NIV) reminds us, "Start children off on the way they should go, and even when they are old they will not turn from it." Our efforts to nurture their spiritual growth will yield a legacy of faith and character that endures through generations.

Chapter 4

The Role of Discipline Biblical Guidelines and Practical Applications

Parenting with Purpose: Character Development Through Faith

Discipline is a critical component of effective parenting, providing children with the structure and guidance they need to develop self-control, responsibility, and respect for others. Proverbs 29:17 (NIV) states, "Discipline your children, and they will give you peace; they will bring you the delights you desire." When approached with love and consistency, discipline becomes a powerful tool for teaching and nurturing our children.

Biblical Principles of Discipline

The Bible offers clear principles for discipline, emphasizing the importance of correction, instruction, and love. Hebrews 12:11 (NIV) acknowledges, "No discipline seems pleasant at the time, but painful. Later on, however, it produces a harvest of righteousness and peace for those who have been trained by it." Discipline, though sometimes challenging, ultimately yields positive outcomes in our children's lives.

Parenting with Purpose: Character Development Through Faith

Correction with Love: Discipline should always be administered with love and a desire to guide, rather than to punish. Ephesians 6:4 (NIV) instructs, "Fathers, do not exasperate your children; instead, bring them up in the training and instruction of the Lord." Our goal is to correct behavior while nurturing their growth and well-being.

Consistency and Fairness: Consistency in discipline helps children understand expectations and consequences. Colossians 3:21 (NIV) advises, "Fathers, do not embitter your children, or they will become discouraged." Fair and consistent discipline fosters a sense of security and trust.

Teaching and Instruction: Discipline should be accompanied by teaching and instruction, helping children understand the reasons behind rules and consequences. Proverbs 13:24 (NIV) states, "Whoever spares the rod hates their children, but the one who loves their children is careful to discipline them." Effective discipline involves guiding children towards understanding and applying biblical principles.

Parenting with Purpose:
Character Development Through Faith

Practical Strategies for Discipline

Establish Clear Rules and Expectations: Set clear, age-appropriate rules and expectations for behavior. Communicate these guidelines to your children, ensuring they understand what is expected of them.

Consistent Consequences: Implement consistent consequences for misbehavior. Ensure that the consequences are fair and proportionate to the offense. Consistency reinforces the importance of adhering to established rules.

Positive Reinforcement: Use positive reinforcement to encourage desirable behavior. Praise and rewards for good behavior can motivate children to continue making positive choices.

Time-Outs and Reflection: For younger children, time-outs can be an effective disciplinary tool. Provide a designated space where they can reflect on their behavior and calm down before rejoining activities.

Natural Consequences: Allow children to experience the natural consequences of their actions when appropriate. This helps them understand the real-life impact of their choices.

Restorative Discipline: Encourage children to make amends for their mistakes. This could involve apologizing, repairing something they broke, or performing a helpful task. Restorative discipline teaches accountability and empathy.

Balancing Discipline with Grace

Discipline must be balanced with grace, ensuring that children feel loved and valued even when they make mistakes. Colossians 3:13 (NIV) reminds us, "Bear with each other and forgive one another if any of you has a grievance against someone. Forgive as the Lord forgave you." Extend grace and forgiveness, helping children learn from their mistakes without feeling condemned.

Communicate Love: After disciplining, reaffirm your love for your child. Ensure they understand that discipline is a form of guidance and not a withdrawal of your affection.

Teach Forgiveness: Model forgiveness by showing grace when children apologize and make amends. Help them understand the importance of forgiving others as well.

Encourage Growth: Use disciplinary moments as opportunities for teaching and growth. Discuss what can be learned from the situation and how they can make better choices in the future.

Conclusion

The role of discipline in parenting is to guide, correct, and nurture our children, helping them develop self-control, responsibility, and respect. By adhering to biblical principles and practical strategies, we can discipline with love and consistency, fostering a positive and supportive environment. As Proverbs 29:17 (NIV) reminds us, "Discipline your children, and they will give you peace; they will bring you the delights you desire." Through thoughtful and loving discipline, we prepare our children to navigate life with wisdom and integrity.

Chapter 6

Encouraging Educational Success

Tailoring Learning Approaches

Education is a vital aspect of a child's development, shaping their intellectual abilities, critical thinking skills, and future opportunities. Proverbs 4:7 (NIV) emphasizes the importance of wisdom: "The beginning of wisdom is this: Get wisdom. Though it cost all you have, get understanding." As parents, we play a crucial role in encouraging our children's educational success by tailoring learning approaches to meet their unique needs. It is our role to foster our children's natural curiosity and journey of self-discovery. Through the process of wisdom and understanding, we gain a sense of self. As a parent, it is a part of our role to help our children reach a place of self discovery and understanding. Learning is life-long and truly foundational in the journey through life.

Understanding Learning Styles

Children have diverse learning styles, and understanding how they learn best is key to supporting their academic growth. The primary learning styles include visual, auditory, kinesthetic, and reading/writing. Recognizing your child's preferred learning style helps you provide effective support and resources.

Parenting with Purpose:
Character Development Through Faith

Visual Learners: "Fix these words of mine in your hearts and minds; tie them as symbols on your hands and bind them on your foreheads." (Deuteronomy 11:18, NIV) Visual learners understand and remember information better when it is presented in a visual format such as diagrams, charts, and pictures. Recognizing this learning style helps educators and parents use visual aids to improve comprehension and retention. Visual learners thrive on seeing and visualizing information. They often remember what they see more than what they hear. This style aligns with how God instructed the Israelites to use visual symbols as reminders of His commandments,

In a history lesson, use timelines and maps to help visual learners understand historical events and geographical locations. Provide illustrated Bible stories or use visual symbols to represent key biblical concepts, aiding in memorization and understanding. Encourage the use of color-coded notes and mind maps to organize information visually, making it easier to study and recall.

Auditory Learners: Auditory learners benefit from listening to information. Support their learning with audiobooks, recorded lectures, and discussions. Encourage them to read aloud and participate in group study sessions. "So then faith comes by hearing, and hearing by the word of God." (Romans 10:17, NKJV) Auditory learners benefit from listening and engaging in discussions. They understand and retain information better when it is heard, making it essential to incorporate auditory elements in teaching. Auditory learners process information through listening. They benefit from oral instructions, discussions, and audio resources. The scripture emphasizes the power of hearing God's word, illustrating the importance of auditory learning in gaining faith and understanding.

Read textbooks or stories aloud to auditory learners. Encourage them to read their notes aloud when studying. Engage auditory learners in group discussions or debates, helping them articulate their thoughts and reinforce learning through dialogue. Utilize audiobooks, podcasts, and recorded lectures to supplement learning materials.

Parenting with Purpose:
Character Development Through Faith

Kinesthetic Learners: These children thrive through hands-on activities and movement. Incorporate physical activities into their learning, such as experiments, models, and interactive lessons. "Whatever you do, work at it with all your heart, as working for the Lord, not for human masters." (Colossians 3:23, NIV) Kinesthetic learners need to engage in physical activities to grasp concepts better. Incorporating movement and hands-on activities into teaching can significantly enhance their learning experience. Kinesthetic learners excel through doing and experiencing. They learn best when they can touch, manipulate, and actively engage with the material. The verse encourages active, wholehearted engagement in all tasks, reflecting the kinesthetic approach to learning by doing.

In science, allow kinesthetic learners to participate in experiments, model building, or practical demonstrations. Integrate movement into lessons, such as using role-play in literature or acting out historical events. Use tools like flashcards, puzzles, and models that kinesthetic learners can manipulate to understand abstract concepts.

Parenting with Purpose:
Character Development Through Faith

Linguistic Learners: These learners prefer reading and writing as their primary modes of learning. Provide ample opportunities for reading, writing essays, and taking detailed notes. "Blessed is the one who reads aloud the words of this prophecy, and blessed are those who hear it and take to heart what is written in it." (Revelation 1:3, NIV) Linguistic learners prefer information presented through written words. They excel in reading textbooks, writing notes, and expressing ideas through writing. Linguistic learners engage deeply with text-based information. They benefit from reading and writing as primary methods of learning. The scripture highlights the importance of reading and internalizing written words, aligning with this learning style. When a person writes down information, dreams, goals, desires and develops an action plan in writing, the plan is more likely to manifest as the writer internalizes the information.

Allow language learners to take detailed notes during lectures and encourage them to write summaries of what they have learned. Provide opportunities for essays, reports, and written reflections to help these learners process and express their understanding.   Supply ample reading materials, such as textbooks, articles, and online resources, to cater to their preference for learning through reading.

Creating a Supportive Learning Environment

A supportive learning environment at home fosters a positive attitude towards education and learning. Learning is life-long. Creating a supportive learning environment encourages academic success and learning in everyday life. Here are some strategies to create an effective learning space:

Designated Study Area: Establish a quiet, well-lit study area free from distractions. Ensure the space is equipped with necessary supplies such as books, stationery, and a comfortable chair.

Parenting with Purpose:
Character Development Through Faith

Structured Routine: Develop a structured routine that includes dedicated study time. Consistency helps children develop good study habits and manage their time effectively.

Encouragement and Motivation: Regularly encourage and motivate your children to do their best. Celebrate their achievements and provide positive reinforcement for their efforts. Place positive affirmations and encouraging words in different areas to promote encouragement and motivation.

Resources and Tools: Provide access to educational resources and tools such as books, online learning platforms, and educational apps. These resources can enhance their learning experience and provide additional support. Check for age appropriate materials. Children's brains develop in stages.

Involvement in School Activities

Active involvement in your child's school activities demonstrates your commitment to their education and helps you stay informed about their progress. Here are some ways to be involved:

Parenting with Purpose:
Character Development Through Faith

Attend Parent-Teacher Meetings: Regularly attend parent-teacher meetings to discuss your child's progress, strengths, and areas for improvement. Collaborate with teachers to develop strategies that support your child's learning.

Volunteer at School, Church or in the Community: Volunteer for school activities and events. Your presence and working alongside children shows your support and provides opportunities to engage with teachers, parents and community members.

Support Extracurricular Activities: Encourage your child's participation in extracurricular activities such as sports, music, and clubs. These activities contribute to their overall development, provide opportunities for social interaction and foster skill and talent discovery and development. .

Encouraging a Love for Learning

Instilling a love for learning in your children helps them develop a lifelong passion for knowledge and growth. Here are some ways to nurture their curiosity and enthusiasm:

Explore Interests: Encourage your children to explore their interests and passions. Provide opportunities for them to delve into subjects that fascinate them, whether it's science, art, or literature.

Foster Curiosity: Promote curiosity by asking open-ended questions and encouraging them to seek answers. Create a culture of inquiry and exploration at home.

Model Lifelong Learning: Demonstrate a love for learning in your own life. Share your own learning experiences and show enthusiasm for acquiring new knowledge and skills.

Read Together: Reading together fosters a love for books and enhances language skills. Make reading a regular part of your family's routine.

Addressing Academic Challenges

Children may encounter academic challenges, and it's important to address these difficulties with patience and support. Here are some strategies to help your child overcome academic obstacles:

Parenting with Purpose:
Character Development Through Faith

Identify the Issue: Identify the specific challenges your child is facing, whether it's a particular subject, learning difficulty, or lack of motivation.

Seek Support: Collaborate with teachers, tutors, or educational specialists to provide additional support and resources. Specialized assistance can help address learning difficulties and improve performance.

Encourage Perseverance: Teach your children the value of perseverance

and resilience. Encourage them to keep trying, even when faced with setbacks.

Focus on Strengths: Emphasize your child's strengths and achievements. Building on their strengths boosts confidence and motivates them to tackle challenging areas.

Conclusion

Encouraging educational success involves understanding your child's unique learning style, creating a supportive learning environment, and actively engaging in their educational journey. By fostering a love for learning and addressing academic challenges with patience and support, we can help our children reach their full potential. Proverbs 4:7 (NIV) reminds us, "The beginning of wisdom is this: Get wisdom. Though it cost all you have, get understanding." As we guide our children towards educational success, we equip them with the knowledge and skills to navigate their future with confidence and wisdom.

Chapter 6

Building Strong Family Relationships

*Parenting with Purpose:
Character Development Through Faith*

The Foundation of a Healthy Home

Strong family relationships form the cornerstone of a healthy and nurturing home environment. Psalm 133:1 (NIV) declares, "How good and pleasant it is when God's people live together in unity!" Building strong bonds within the family fosters a sense of belonging, security, and love, creating a solid foundation for children to thrive.

The Importance of Communication

Effective communication is essential for building strong family relationships. Open and honest communication fosters understanding, resolves conflicts, and strengthens connections. Ephesians 4:29 (NIV) advises, "Do not let any unwholesome talk come out of your mouths, but only what is helpful for building others up according to their needs, that it may benefit those who listen."

Active Listening: Practice active listening by giving full attention to each family member when they speak. Show empathy and understanding, validating their feelings and perspectives.

Expressing Feelings: Encourage family members to express their feelings openly and respectfully. Create a safe space where everyone feels comfortable sharing their thoughts and emotions.

Regular Check-Ins: Schedule regular family check-ins to discuss everyone's well-being, address concerns, and celebrate achievements. These check-ins strengthen family bonds and ensure everyone feels heard and supported.

Quality Time and Shared Activities

Spending quality time together as a family strengthens relationships and creates lasting memories. Shared activities foster connection and provide opportunities for bonding. Deuteronomy 6:7 (NIV) emphasizes the importance of spending time together: "Impress them on your children. Talk about them when you sit at home and when you walk along the road, when you lie down and when you get up."

1. Family Meals: Share regular family meals, creating an opportunity to connect and communicate. Mealtime conversations can strengthen family bonds and provide a sense of togetherness.
2. Fun Activities: Engage in fun activities that everyone enjoys, such as playing games, going on outings, or pursuing hobbies together. These activities create positive experiences and reinforce family unity.

Family Traditions: Establish family traditions that provide a sense of continuity and belonging. Traditions, whether daily, weekly, or annual, create cherished memories and strengthen family identity.

Conflict Resolution and Forgiveness

Conflicts are a natural part of family life, and learning to resolve them constructively is crucial for maintaining harmony. Colossians 3:13 (NIV) reminds us, "Bear with each other and forgive one another if any of you has a grievance against someone. Forgive as the Lord forgave you."

Addressing Conflicts: Address conflicts promptly and calmly. Encourage open communication and active listening to understand each other's perspectives.

Finding Solutions: Work together to find mutually acceptable solutions. Compromise and collaboration foster a sense of fairness and respect.

Practicing Forgiveness: Emphasize the importance of forgiveness and grace. Teach children to forgive and seek forgiveness, reinforcing the value of reconciliation.

Building Trust and Respect

Trust and respect are foundational elements of strong family relationships. Ephesians 4:2 (NIV) advises, "Be completely humble and gentle; be patient, bearing with one another in love."

Trustworthiness: Build trust by being reliable, honest, and consistent. Trust is earned through actions that demonstrate care and integrity.

Parenting with Purpose: Character Development Through Faith

Respecting Boundaries: Respect each family member's boundaries and individuality. Encourage mutual respect and consideration for each other's needs and preferences.

Supporting Each Other: Provide support and encouragement in both good times and challenging times. Being there for each other strengthens trust and deepens connections.

Cultivating a Culture of Gratitude

Gratitude fosters a positive and loving atmosphere within the family. Colossians 3:15 (NIV) encourages us, "Let the peace of Christ rule in your hearts, since as members of one body you were called to peace. And be thankful."

Expressing Gratitude: Regularly express gratitude to each family member for their contributions and acts of kindness. Acknowledge and appreciate each other's efforts.

Gratitude Practices: Incorporate gratitude practices into daily routines, such as sharing things you're thankful for during meals or bedtime.

Modeling Gratitude: Demonstrate gratitude in your own actions and attitudes. Let your children see you appreciating life's blessings and expressing thanks.

Conclusion

Building strong family relationships requires intentional effort, effective communication, and a foundation of trust and respect. By spending quality time together, resolving conflicts constructively, and cultivating a culture of gratitude, we create a nurturing and supportive home environment. Psalm 133:1 (NIV) reminds us, "How good and pleasant it is when God's people live together in unity!" As we invest in our family relationships, we lay the groundwork for a healthy and harmonious home where love and unity flourish.

Chapter 7
Balancing Work and Family

*Parenting with Purpose:
Character Development Through Faith*

Finding Harmony in a Busy World

In today's fast-paced world, balancing work and family responsibilities can be challenging. Ecclesiastes 3:1 (NIV) reminds us, "There is a time for everything, and a season for every activity under the heavens." Finding harmony between professional and family life requires intentionality, prioritization, and a commitment to creating a balanced lifestyle.

Setting Priorities

Establishing clear priorities is essential for achieving a healthy work-life balance. Matthew 6:33 (NIV) advises, "But seek first his kingdom and his righteousness, and all these things will be given to you as well." By prioritizing our relationship with God, our family, and our work, we can create a balanced and fulfilling life.

God First: Make your relationship with God the top priority. Spend time in prayer, Bible study, and worship, seeking His guidance and wisdom in all aspects of life.

Family Second: Prioritize your family, ensuring that they receive your time, attention, and love. Make family time a non-negotiable part of your daily routine.

Work Third: While work is important, it should not overshadow your relationship with God and your family. Strive to maintain a healthy boundary between work and personal life.

Time Management and Organization

Effective time management and organization are crucial for balancing work and family responsibilities. 1 Corinthians 14:49 (NIV) states "But everything should be done in a fitting and orderly way." Ephesians 5:15-16 (NIV) encourages us, "Be very careful, then, how you live—not as unwise but as wise, making the most of every opportunity, because the days are evil."

Plan Ahead: Create a weekly schedule that includes time for work, family, personal activities, and rest. Planning ahead helps you allocate time effectively and avoid last-minute stress.

***Parenting with Purpose:
Character Development Through Faith***

Set Boundaries: Establish clear boundaries between work and family time. Avoid bringing work-related tasks into family time and vice versa.

Delegate Tasks: Delegate tasks at home and work to share the load. Involve family members in household chores and seek support from colleagues for work-related responsibilities.

Quality Time with Family

Spending quality time with family strengthens bonds and creates lasting memories. Prioritize activities that foster connection and joy. Deuteronomy 6:6-7 (NIV) emphasizes the importance of spending time together: "These commandments that I give you today are to be on your hearts. Impress them on your children. Talk about them when you sit at home and when you walk along the road, when you lie down and when you get up."

Family Meals: Share regular family meals to connect and communicate. Use mealtime to discuss daily experiences and share stories.

Fun Activities: Engage in fun and meaningful activities that everyone enjoys. Plan family outings, game nights, and creative projects to build strong connections.

One-on-One Time: Spend individual time with each family member. Personalized attention strengthens relationships and makes each person feel valued.

Managing Work Responsibilities

Balancing work responsibilities with family life requires effective strategies and a proactive approach. Colossians 3:23 (NIV) advises, "Whatever you do, work at it with all your heart, as working for the Lord, not for human masters."

Set Realistic Goals: Set achievable work goals and prioritize tasks based on their importance and deadlines. Avoid overcommitting and manage your workload effectively.

Efficient Work Practices: Implement efficient work practices to maximize productivity. Use tools and techniques that help you stay organized and focused.

Flexible Work Arrangements: If possible, explore flexible work arrangements such as remote work or flexible hours. This can provide more time for family and reduce stress.

Self-Care and Rest

Taking care of yourself is essential for maintaining balance and well-being. Matthew 11:28-30 (NIV) reminds us, "Come to me, all you who are weary and burdened, and I will give you rest. Take my yoke upon you and learn from me, for I am gentle and humble in heart, and you will find rest for your souls. For my yoke is easy and my burden is light."

Prioritize Self-Care: Make time for self-care activities that rejuvenate and energize you. This can include exercise, hobbies, relaxation, and spiritual practices.

Rest and Rejuvenation: Ensure you get adequate rest and sleep. Rest is crucial for physical, mental, and emotional well-being.

Seek Support: Reach out for support when needed. Whether it's talking to a friend, seeking professional guidance, or asking for help with tasks, don't hesitate to seek assistance.

Conclusion

Balancing work and family requires intentional effort, effective time management, and a commitment to setting priorities. By prioritizing our relationship with God, spending quality time with family, managing work responsibilities efficiently, and taking care of ourselves, we can achieve a harmonious and fulfilling life. Ecclesiastes 3:1 (NIV) reminds us, "There is a time for everything, and a season for every activity under the heavens." As we navigate the demands of work and family, we can find balance and peace in God's guidance and grace.

Chapter 8

Fostering Character Development

Parenting with Purpose:
Character Development Through Faith

Raising Children with Integrity

Character development is a fundamental aspect of parenting, shaping our children's values, behavior, and moral compass. Proverbs 22:1 (NIV) states, "A good name is more desirable than great riches; to be esteemed is better than silver or gold." Instilling integrity and strong character in our children equips them to navigate life with honesty, responsibility, and compassion.

The Role of Role Modeling

Children learn by observing the behavior and attitudes of their parents. Role modeling is a powerful tool for teaching character and values. Titus 2:7-8 (NIV) advises, "In everything set them an example by doing what is good. In your teaching show integrity, seriousness and soundness of speech that cannot be condemned."

Demonstrate Integrity: Model integrity in your actions and decisions. Show honesty, transparency, and ethical behavior in your daily life.

*Parenting with Purpose:
Character Development Through Faith*

Practice Kindness: Demonstrate kindness and compassion in your interactions with others. Acts of kindness leave a lasting impression on children and teach them to value empathy.

Show Respect: Treat others with respect and dignity. Modeling respectful behavior teaches children to value and practice respect in their relationships.

Teaching Core Values

Teaching core values provides a foundation for strong character development. These values guide children in making ethical decisions and developing a moral compass. Deuteronomy 6:6-7 (NIV) emphasizes the importance of teaching values: "These commandments that I give you today are to be on your hearts. Impress them on your children. Talk about them when you sit at home and when you walk along the road, when you lie down and when you get up." In context, Deuteronomy is 6:6-7 is referring to the information shared in Deuteronomy 5:6-2. These are the ten commandments given to Moses on Mount Sinah. It is the foundation to core values, character and principle teaching with regards to relationships with others.

Parenting with Purpose:
Character Development Through Faith

Honesty: Teach the importance of honesty and truthfulness. Encourage children to always tell the truth, even when it's difficult.

Responsibility: Instill a sense of responsibility by assigning age-appropriate tasks and chores. Teach children to take ownership of their actions and obligations.

Compassion: Foster compassion by encouraging empathy and understanding. Discuss the importance of helping others and showing kindness.

Perseverance: Encourage perseverance and resilience in the face of challenges. Teach children the value of hard work and determination.

Encouraging Ethical Decision-Making

Helping children develop ethical decision-making skills equips them to navigate complex situations with integrity. Proverbs 11:3 (NIV) reminds us, "The integrity of the upright guides them, but the unfaithful are destroyed by their duplicity."

Discuss Scenarios: Discuss hypothetical scenarios that require ethical decision-making. Encourage children to think through the consequences of different choices.

Reflect on Choices: After a decision has been made, reflect on the process and outcomes. Discuss what was learned and how it can inform future decisions.

Provide Guidance: Offer guidance and support when children face ethical dilemmas. Help them consider their values and the impact of their choices on others.

Reinforcing Positive Behavior

Reinforcing positive behavior encourages children to continue making good choices and developing strong character. Hebrews 10:24 (NIV) advises, "And let us consider how we may spur one another on toward love and good deeds."

Praise and Recognition: Praise and recognize positive behavior and acts of integrity. Affirmation reinforces the value of making good choices.

Positive Reinforcement: Use positive reinforcement techniques such as rewards and incentives to encourage desirable behavior.

Celebrate Achievements: Celebrate achievements and milestones in character development. Acknowledge the effort and growth that contributed to these accomplishments.

Addressing Mistakes and Learning Opportunities

Mistakes are valuable learning opportunities that contribute to character development. Proverbs 24:16 (NIV) reminds us, "For though the righteous fall seven times, they rise again, but the wicked stumble when calamity strikes." This verse highlights the resilience and determination of the righteous. It reminds us that making mistakes is a natural part of life, but what truly matters is our ability to rise again and learn from those mistakes. This perspective encourages a growth mindset, where failures are seen as stepping stones to success rather than setbacks.

Parenting with Purpose:
Character Development Through Faith

Encourage Accountability: "Each one should test their own actions. Then they can take pride in themselves alone, without comparing themselves to someone else." (Galatians 6:4, NIV) Encourage children to take responsibility for their mistakes. Discuss what went wrong and how they can learn from the experience. Suppose a child forgot to do their homework and got a poor grade as a result. Instead of making excuses, encourage them to acknowledge the mistake. Have a conversation about why the homework was missed and discuss strategies to remember it next time, such as setting reminders or organizing their study schedule better. Teaching accountability helps children understand that their actions have consequences. It promotes honesty and integrity, show

Parenting with Purpose:
Character Development Through Faith

Provide Constructive Feedback: Offer constructive feedback that focuses on improvement and growth. "Therefore encourage one another and build each other up, just as in fact you are doing." (1 Thessalonians 5:11, NIV) If a child receives a low grade on a test, instead of saying, "You should have studied harder," try, "Let's review the areas you found difficult and work on them together for next time." This approach encourages them to see the mistake as a learning opportunity rather than a failure.

Constructive feedback helps children focus on what they can do better next time, fostering a positive attitude towards learning and self-improvement. It helps them understand that mistakes are part of the learning process and that effort and persistence can lead to improvement. Avoid criticism that may discourage or shame them.

Teach Forgiveness: Teach the importance of forgiveness and grace. "Be kind and compassionate to one another, forgiving each other, just as in Christ God forgave you." (Ephesians 4:32, NIV) Model forgiving behavior and encourage children to forgive themselves and others. If a child accidentally breaks a sibling's toy, encourage the sibling to forgive them and discuss ways to make amends, like helping with chores or sharing their own toys. Also, emphasize that it's important for the child who made the mistake to forgive themselves and learn to be more careful in the future.

Teaching forgiveness helps children understand that everyone makes mistakes and that forgiving others is a way to move forward positively. It also teaches them to be kind to themselves, reducing feelings of guilt and promoting emotional well-being.

Conclusion

Fostering character development in children is a vital aspect of parenting, shaping their values, behavior, and ethical decision-making. By role modeling integrity, teaching core values, encouraging ethical choices, reinforcing positive behavior, and addressing mistakes constructively, we guide our children in developing strong character. Proverbs 22:1 (NIV) reminds us, "A good name is more desirable than great riches; to be esteemed is better than silver or gold." As we nurture our children's character, we equip them to navigate life with integrity, compassion, and responsibility.

Chapter 9

Encouraging Creativity and Self-Expression

*Parenting with Purpose:
Character Development Through Faith*

Nurturing the Unique Gifts of Each Child

Creativity and self-expression are essential components of a child's development, allowing them to explore their unique talents, interests, and perspectives. Psalm 139:14 (NIV) declares, "I praise you because I am fearfully and wonderfully made; your works are wonderful, I know that full well." Encouraging creativity and self-expression fosters a sense of individuality and confidence in children, helping them discover and embrace their God-given gifts.

Creating an Environment that Fosters Creativity

Creating an environment that nurtures creativity involves providing opportunities, resources, and encouragement for children to explore their interests and express themselves. Ephesians 2:10 (NIV) reminds us, "For we are God's handiwork, created in Christ Jesus to do good works, which God prepared in advance for us to do."

Provide Resources: Offer a variety of resources such as art supplies, musical instruments, books, and building materials. Access to diverse tools and materials encourages exploration and creativity.

Encourage Exploration: Allow children to explore different activities and interests. Encourage them to try new things and discover what they enjoy and excel at.

Create a Safe Space: Create a safe and supportive environment where children feel comfortable expressing themselves without fear of judgment or criticism.

Encouraging Artistic Expression

Artistic expression provides children with a powerful outlet for creativity and self-discovery. Whether through visual arts, music, dance, or drama, artistic activities help children develop their unique voice and perspective.

Art and Crafts: Provide opportunities for drawing, painting, sculpting, and crafting. Encourage children to experiment with different techniques and materials.

Music and Dance: Support musical interests by offering access to instruments, music lessons, and opportunities to perform. Encourage dancing and movement as a form of expression and joy.

Drama and Performance: Encourage participation in drama and performance activities such as theater, storytelling, and public speaking. These activities build confidence and communication skills.

Supporting Creative Thinking and Problem-Solving

Creative thinking and problem-solving skills are essential for navigating life's challenges and opportunities. Encouraging children to think creatively and approach problems with an open mind fosters innovation and resilience.

Open-Ended Questions: Ask open-ended questions that stimulate creative thinking and exploration. Encourage children to think critically and come up with multiple solutions to problems.

Brainstorming Sessions: Conduct brainstorming sessions where children can freely share ideas and collaborate on projects. This fosters a sense of teamwork and innovation.

Real-World Challenges: Present real-world challenges and encourage children to develop creative solutions. This practical application of creativity enhances problem-solving skills.

Nurturing Individuality and Self-Expression

Nurturing individuality and self-expression involves recognizing and celebrating each child's unique gifts and talents. Psalm 139:14 (NIV) reminds us of the value of individuality: "I praise you because I am fearfully and wonderfully made; your works are wonderful, I know that full well."

Celebrate Differences: Celebrate and appreciate the unique qualities and talents of each child. Encourage them to embrace their individuality and express themselves authentically.

Support Interests: Support and nurture children's interests and passions. Provide opportunities for them to pursue activities that resonate with their unique talents.

Encourage Self-Expression: Encourage children to express themselves through their words, actions, and creative endeavors. Validate their feelings and perspectives, fostering a sense of confidence and self-worth.

Balancing Structure and Freedom

Balancing structure and freedom is essential for fostering creativity while providing the guidance and support children need. Proverbs 22:6 (NIV) advises, "Start children off on the way they should go, and even when they are old they will not turn from it."

Provide Guidance: Offer guidance and support while allowing children the freedom to explore and experiment. Strike a balance between structured activities and open-ended play.

Set Boundaries: Establish clear boundaries and expectations that provide a sense of security and direction. Within these boundaries, encourage children to take creative risks and express themselves freely.

Encourage Independence: Encourage independence and self-directed learning. Allow children to take ownership of their creative projects and make decisions about their work.

Conclusion

Encouraging creativity and self-expression nurtures the unique gifts of each child, fostering a sense of individuality and confidence. By creating an environment that supports artistic expression, creative thinking, and problem-solving, we help children discover and embrace their God-given talents. Psalm 139:14 (NIV) reminds us, "I praise you because I am fearfully and wonderfully made; your works are wonderful, I know that full well." As we celebrate and nurture our children's creativity, we empower them to explore their unique gifts and contribute their creativity to the world.

Chapter 10

Instilling Faith and Spiritual Values

Parenting with Purpose:
Character Development Through Faith

Guiding Children on Their Spiritual Journey

Instilling faith and spiritual values in children is a vital aspect of parenting that provides a foundation for their moral and spiritual development. Proverbs 22:6 (NIV) emphasizes, "Start children off on the way they should go, and even when they are old they will not turn from it." Guiding children on their spiritual journey involves teaching them about God's love, fostering a personal relationship with Him, and encouraging them to live according to His principles.

Teaching Biblical Principles

Teaching biblical principles helps children understand God's teachings and how to apply them in their daily lives. Deuteronomy 6:6-7 (NIV) instructs, "These commandments that I give you today are to be on your hearts. Impress them on your children. Talk about them when you sit at home and when you walk along the road, when you lie down and when you get up."

Daily Devotions: Incorporate daily devotions and Bible readings into your family routine. Discuss the passages and their relevance to everyday life.

Memorize Scripture: Encourage children to memorize Bible verses. This practice helps them internalize God's Word and recall His teachings in various situations.

Practical Application: Teach children how to apply biblical principles in real-life scenarios. Discuss how God's teachings guide their actions and decisions.

Fostering a Personal Relationship with God

Fostering a personal relationship with God involves encouraging children to seek Him, pray, and develop a deep, personal connection with Him. James 4:8 (NIV) promises, "Come near to God and he will come near to you."

Prayer Life: Teach children the importance of prayer and how to communicate with God. Encourage them to pray regularly, sharing their thoughts, feelings, and requests with Him.

Worship: Engage in regular worship as a family. Attend church services, participate in worship activities, and praise God together.

Parenting with Purpose:
Character Development Through Faith

Spiritual Guidance: Provide spiritual guidance and mentorship. Share your own faith journey, experiences, and the ways you seek God's presence in your life.

Living Out Faith through Actions

Living out faith through actions demonstrates to children how to embody God's love and principles in their daily interactions and decisions. Matthew 5:16 (NIV) encourages, "In the same way, let your light shine before others, that they may see your good deeds and glorify your Father in heaven."

Acts of Kindness: Encourage children to perform acts of kindness and service. Model compassion and generosity, showing them how to serve others selflessly.

Ethical Living: Teach children to live ethically and make choices that reflect their faith. Discuss moral dilemmas and how to navigate them with integrity.

Community Involvement: Involve children in church and community activities. Participation in faith-based initiatives reinforces the importance of living out their beliefs.

Parenting with Purpose:
Character Development Through Faith

Nurturing a Heart for Worship

Nurturing a heart for worship involves fostering a love for praising and glorifying God through music, prayer, and communal worship experiences. Psalm 95:1 (NIV) invites, "Come, let us sing for joy to the Lord; let us shout aloud to the Rock of our salvation."

Music and Worship: Incorporate music and worship into your family life. Sing worship songs, play instruments, and create a joyful atmosphere of praise.

Family Worship Time: Set aside regular family worship time. Engage in singing, prayer, and reflection together, deepening your collective connection to God.

Church Involvement: Encourage active participation in church worship services. Foster a sense of belonging and commitment to the faith community.

Addressing Spiritual Questions and Doubts

Addressing spiritual questions and doubts is an important part of nurturing a child's faith. Encourage open dialogue and provide thoughtful, honest answers to their inquiries. 1 Peter 3:15 (NIV) advises, "But in your hearts revere Christ as Lord. Always be prepared to give an answer to everyone who asks you to give the reason for the hope that you have."

Open Dialogue: Create a safe space for children to ask questions and express doubts. Listen actively and respond with empathy and understanding.

Explore Together: Explore spiritual questions together by studying the Bible, reading faith-based books, and seeking guidance from trusted spiritual leaders.

Encourage Faith Exploration: Encourage children to explore their faith independently. Support their journey of discovery and growth, providing resources and encouragement.

Parenting with Purpose:
Character Development Through Faith

Leading by Example

Leading by example is one of the most powerful ways to instill faith and spiritual values in children. Demonstrating a life rooted in faith inspires children to follow your example. 1 Corinthians 11:1 (NIV) urges, "Follow my example, as I follow the example of Christ."

Consistent Faith Practice: Live out your faith consistently in daily life. Show how your beliefs influence your decisions, actions, and interactions.

Authenticity: Be authentic in your faith journey. Share your struggles, doubts, and triumphs, demonstrating that faith is a dynamic and evolving relationship with God.

Spiritual Leadership: Take on a spiritual leadership role within the family. Guide, support, and nurture your children's faith with wisdom and love.

Conclusion

Instilling faith and spiritual values in children provides them with a solid foundation for their moral and spiritual development. By teaching biblical principles, fostering a personal relationship with God, living out faith through actions, nurturing a heart for worship, addressing spiritual questions, and leading by example, we guide our children on their spiritual journey. Proverbs 22:6 (NIV) reminds us, "Start children off on the way they should go, and even when they are old they will not turn from it." As we invest in our children's spiritual growth, we equip them to live lives rooted in faith, love, and integrity.

Chapter 11
Navigating Adolescence

*Parenting with Purpose:
Character Development Through Faith*

Guiding Teens through a Critical Life Stage

Adolescence is a pivotal stage of development marked by significant physical, emotional, and social changes. Proverbs 3:5-6 (NIV) offers timeless wisdom for this period: "Trust in the Lord with all your heart and lean not on your own understanding; in all your ways submit to him, and he will make your paths straight." Guiding teens through adolescence requires patience, understanding, and a balance of support and independence.

Understanding Adolescent Development

Understanding the developmental changes teens undergo is crucial for effective guidance. Adolescence involves rapid physical growth, cognitive development, and emotional maturation.

Physical Changes: Adolescents experience significant physical changes, including puberty, which can impact their self-image and confidence. Provide reassurance and accurate information about these changes.

Cognitive Development: Teens develop advanced cognitive abilities, including abstract thinking and problem-solving. Encourage critical thinking and support their intellectual growth.

Emotional Maturity: Emotional regulation becomes more complex during adolescence. Help teens navigate their emotions by offering support, empathy, and guidance.

Building Trust and Communication

Building trust and maintaining open communication are essential for guiding teens. James 1:19 (NIV) advises, "Everyone should be quick to listen, slow to speak and slow to become angry."

Active Listening: Practice active listening by giving your full attention to your teen's thoughts and feelings. Validate their experiences and show empathy.

Parenting with Purpose:
Character Development Through Faith

Open Dialogue: Encourage open dialogue about various topics, including challenges, goals, and values. Create a safe space where teens feel comfortable sharing without fear of judgment.

Honesty and Transparency: Be honest and transparent with your teens. Share your own experiences and values, fostering a relationship built on trust and mutual respect.

Encouraging Independence and Responsibility

Encouraging independence and responsibility helps teens develop the skills needed for adulthood. Proverbs 16:3 (NIV) advises, "Commit to the Lord whatever you do, and he will establish your plans."

Decision-Making: Involve teens in decision-making processes. Encourage them to weigh options, consider consequences, and make informed choices.

Responsibility: Assign age-appropriate responsibilities and chores. Teach teens the importance of accountability and the value of contributing to the family and community.

Goal Setting: Help teens set realistic and achievable goals. Support their aspirations and provide guidance on how to pursue their dreams effectively.

Navigating Peer Relationships and Social Pressures

Peer relationships and social pressures are significant aspects of adolescence. Proverbs 13:20 (NIV) reminds us, "Walk with the wise and become wise, for a companion of fools suffers harm."

Healthy Friendships: Encourage teens to build healthy and positive friendships. Discuss the qualities of a good friend and the importance of mutual respect and support.

Handling Peer Pressure: Equip teens with strategies to handle peer pressure. Role-play scenarios and discuss how to make decisions aligned with their values.

Social Skills: Teach essential social skills, including communication, empathy, and conflict resolution. These skills help teens navigate complex social dynamics.

Parenting with Purpose:
Character Development Through Faith

Supporting Academic and Extracurricular Involvement

Supporting teens' academic and extracurricular involvement fosters a sense of accomplishment and purpose. Colossians 3:23 (NIV) advises, "Whatever you do, work at it with all your heart, as working for the Lord, not for human masters."

Academic Support: Provide academic support and encouragement. Help teens develop effective study habits, time management skills, and a positive attitude toward learning.

Extracurricular Activities: Encourage participation in extracurricular activities that align with their interests and talents. These activities provide opportunities for skill development and social engagement.

Balanced Schedule: Help teens balance their academic, extracurricular, and personal responsibilities. Ensure they have time for relaxation, hobbies, and family activities.

Addressing Mental Health and Well-Being

Addressing mental health and well-being is crucial during adolescence. Philippians 4:6-7 (NIV) offers comfort: "Do not be anxious about anything, but in every situation, by prayer and petition, with thanksgiving, present your requests to God. And the peace of God, which transcends all understanding, will guard your hearts and your minds in Christ Jesus."

Mental Health Awareness: Promote awareness of mental health and well-being. Discuss the importance of self-care, stress management, and seeking help when needed.

Professional Support: Seek professional support if needed. Mental health professionals can provide guidance and interventions for teens facing significant challenges.

Emotional Support: Offer emotional support and understanding. Be available to listen, provide comfort, and help teens navigate their feelings and experiences.

Conclusion

Navigating adolescence is a critical aspect of parenting that requires patience, understanding, and guidance. By understanding adolescent development, building trust and communication, encouraging independence and responsibility, navigating peer relationships, supporting academic and extracurricular involvement, and addressing mental health and well-being, we can effectively guide teens through this transformative stage. Proverbs 3:5-6 (NIV) reminds us to trust in the Lord and seek His guidance in all our ways. As we support our teens on their journey, we equip them to grow into confident, responsible, and spiritually grounded individuals.

*Parenting with Purpose:
Character Development Through Faith*

Preparing for Adulthood

Chapter 12

Equipping Young Adults for Independent Living

Preparing children for adulthood involves equipping them with the skills, knowledge, and values needed for independent living. Proverbs 22:6 (NIV) states, "Start children off on the way they should go, and even when they are old they will not turn from it." This chapter focuses on helping young adults transition from adolescence to adulthood with confidence and competence.

Developing Life Skills

Developing essential life skills is crucial for young adults to navigate the complexities of independent living. These skills include financial management, time management, and practical daily living skills.

Financial Literacy: Teach young adults about budgeting, saving, investing, and managing expenses. Encourage them to develop a responsible approach to money management.

Time Management: Help young adults develop effective time management skills. Encourage them to prioritize tasks, set goals, and create schedules that balance work, study, and personal time.

Practical Skills: Ensure young adults are proficient in practical skills such as cooking, cleaning, laundry, and basic home maintenance. These skills are essential for self-sufficiency.

Career and Education Planning

Career and education planning involves guiding young adults in making informed decisions about their future paths. Jeremiah 29:11 (NIV) offers reassurance: "For I know the plans I have for you," declares the Lord, "plans to prosper you and not to harm you, plans to give you hope and a future."

Career Exploration: Encourage young adults to explore different career options. Discuss their interests, strengths, and goals, and provide resources for career research and exploration.

Education and Training: Support young adults in pursuing further education and training. Discuss options such as college, vocational training, apprenticeships, and online courses.

Goal Setting: Help young adults set realistic and achievable career and education goals. Provide guidance on how to create action plans and pursue their aspirations.

Building Healthy Relationships

Building healthy relationships is fundamental for personal and professional success. Ephesians 4:2-3 (NIV) advises, "Be completely humble and gentle; be patient, bearing with one another in love. Make every effort to keep the unity of the Spirit through the bond of peace."

Communication Skills: Teach young adults effective communication skills, including active listening, assertiveness, and conflict resolution. These skills are vital for healthy relationships.

Boundaries and Respect: Discuss the importance of setting and respecting boundaries in relationships. Encourage young adults to establish healthy boundaries in personal and professional interactions.

Networking: Emphasize the value of networking and building professional relationships. Encourage young adults to seek mentorship and connect with individuals in their desired fields.

Cultivating Emotional and Mental Well-Being

Cultivating emotional and mental well-being is essential for a balanced and fulfilling life. Philippians 4:6-7 (NIV) offers comfort: "Do not be anxious about anything, but in every situation, by prayer and petition, with thanksgiving, present your requests to God. And the peace of God, which transcends all understanding, will guard your hearts and your minds in Christ Jesus."

Self-Care: Encourage young adults to prioritize self-care activities that promote emotional and mental well-being. This includes exercise, hobbies, relaxation, and spiritual practices.

Stress Management: Teach stress management techniques such as mindfulness, meditation, and time management. Help young adults develop healthy coping strategies for dealing with stress.

Support Systems: Encourage young adults to build strong support systems. This includes maintaining relationships with family, friends, mentors, and seeking professional help when needed.

Nurturing Spiritual Growth

Nurturing spiritual growth involves encouraging young adults to deepen their relationship with God and live according to His principles. Psalm 119:105 (NIV) states, "Your word is a lamp for my feet, a light on my path."

Personal Faith Practices: Encourage young adults to engage in personal faith practices such as prayer, Bible study, and worship. These practices strengthen their spiritual foundation.

Parenting with Purpose:
Character Development Through Faith

Community Involvement: Support involvement in church and faith-based communities. Participation in communal worship and service activities fosters spiritual growth and a sense of belonging.

Purpose and Calling: Help young adults discover their purpose and calling. Encourage them to seek God's guidance in their decisions and to live a life that honors Him.

Conclusion

Preparing young adults for adulthood involves equipping them with the skills, knowledge, and values needed for independent living. By developing life skills, planning for career and education, building healthy relationships, cultivating emotional and mental well-being, and nurturing spiritual growth, we guide young adults in their transition to adulthood. Proverbs 22:6 (NIV) reminds us to start children off on the way they should go, ensuring they have a strong foundation for their future. As we support our young adults, we empower them to navigate life with confidence, competence, and faith.

Chapter 13

Embracing Diversity and Inclusion

Teaching Children to Value Differences

Embracing diversity and inclusion is essential for raising children who value and respect the differences in others. Galatians 3:28 (NIV) reminds us, "There is neither Jew nor Gentile, neither slave nor free, nor is there male and female, for you are all one in Christ Jesus." Teaching children to embrace diversity involves promoting acceptance, understanding, and appreciation of different cultures, backgrounds, and perspectives.

Promoting Cultural Awareness

Promoting cultural awareness helps children understand and appreciate the diverse world in which they live. Acts 17:26 (NIV) states, "From one man he made all the nations, that they should inhabit the whole earth; and he marked out their appointed times in history and the boundaries of their lands."

Cultural Education: Provide opportunities for children to learn about different cultures through books, music, art, and food. Discuss the unique customs, traditions, and histories of various cultures.

Diverse Experiences: Encourage children to participate in diverse experiences, such as cultural festivals, international events, and community activities. Exposure to different cultures fosters appreciation and respect.

Family Traditions: Share and celebrate your own cultural traditions with your children. Encourage them to take pride in their heritage while respecting the traditions of others.

Teaching Empathy and Respect

Teaching empathy and respect involves helping children understand and appreciate the feelings and perspectives of others. Romans 12:10 (NIV) advises, "Be devoted to one another in love. Honor one another above yourselves."

Empathy Exercises: Engage in activities that promote empathy, such as role-playing scenarios, reading stories about diverse characters, and discussing feelings and perspectives.

Respectful Communication: Teach children how to communicate respectfully with others, even when they have different opinions. Encourage active listening, patience, and kindness.

Inclusive Language: Use inclusive language that respects and acknowledges the diversity of others. Avoid stereotypes and prejudiced language, and educate children on the impact of their words.

Encouraging Inclusive Behavior

Encouraging inclusive behavior involves teaching children to include and support others, regardless of their differences. Ephesians 4:2-3 (NIV) advises, "Be completely humble and gentle; be patient, bearing with one another in love. Make every effort to keep the unity of the Spirit through the bond of peace."

Inclusive Activities: Encourage children to include others in activities and play. Teach them to be welcoming and supportive of peers who may feel excluded.

Parenting with Purpose:
Character Development Through Faith

Stand Against Bullying: Educate children about the harmful effects of bullying and discrimination. Encourage them to stand up against such behaviors and support those who are marginalized.

Celebrate Diversity: Celebrate diversity within your family and community. Recognize and honor the unique qualities and contributions of each individual.

Addressing Prejudices and Biases

Addressing prejudices and biases is essential for fostering an inclusive mindset. James 2:1 (NIV) warns, "My brothers and sisters, believers in our glorious Lord Jesus Christ must not show favoritism."

Self-Reflection: Encourage self-reflection and discussions about biases and prejudices. Help children recognize and challenge their own assumptions and stereotypes.

Educational Resources: Provide educational resources that address issues of prejudice, discrimination, and social justice. Use books, documentaries, and discussions to raise awareness.

Role Models: Highlight positive role models who promote diversity and inclusion. Share stories of individuals who have made significant contributions to social justice and equality.

Fostering a Sense of Belonging

Fostering a sense of belonging helps children feel valued and accepted within their community. Psalm 133:1 (NIV) states, "How good and pleasant it is when God's people live together in unity!"

Community Involvement: Encourage children to participate in community activities that promote unity and inclusion. Volunteering, group projects, and social events foster a sense of belonging.

Supportive Environment: Create a supportive and inclusive environment at home and in social settings. Ensure that all children feel valued, respected, and included.

Affirmation and Acceptance: Affirm and accept each child's unique qualities and contributions. Celebrate their individuality and encourage them to embrace their identity.

Conclusion

Embracing diversity and inclusion is essential for raising children who value and respect the differences in others. By promoting cultural awareness, teaching empathy and respect, encouraging inclusive behavior, addressing prejudices and biases, and fostering a sense of belonging, we guide our children in embracing diversity. Galatians 3:28 (NIV) reminds us that we are all one in Christ Jesus. As we teach our children to value and celebrate diversity, we prepare them to contribute to a more inclusive and harmonious world.

Chapter 14

Nurturing Faith

Parenting with Purpose:
Character Development Through Faith

Building a Strong Spiritual Foundation

Nurturing faith in children and young adults is essential for building a strong spiritual foundation that guides their values, decisions, and relationships. Proverbs 22:6 (NIV) advises, "Start children off on the way they should go, and even when they are old they will not turn from it." This chapter explores ways to instill a deep, abiding faith in children that will sustain them throughout their lives.

Leading by Example

One of the most effective ways to nurture faith is by leading by example. Children learn a great deal from observing the actions and attitudes of their parents and caregivers.

Daily Devotionals: Incorporate daily devotionals and prayer into your routine. Share scripture and reflections, demonstrating the importance of regular spiritual practice.

Faith in Action: Show how faith influences daily decisions and actions. Discuss how biblical principles guide your choices, fostering an environment where faith is lived out authentically.

Church Involvement: Actively participate in church activities and services as a family. Your commitment to the faith community will encourage your children to value and engage in communal worship.

Encouraging Personal Faith Practices

Encouraging personal faith practices helps children develop their own relationship with God. Philippians 4:13 (NIV) states, "I can do all this through him who gives me strength."

Prayer: Teach children how to pray, emphasizing the importance of communication with God. Encourage them to pray about their joys, struggles, and concerns.

Bible Study: Provide age-appropriate Bible study materials and encourage regular reading. Discuss the lessons and stories, helping them understand and apply biblical principles.

Worship: Encourage personal worship through music, art, and creative expression. Allow children to explore different ways to connect with God and express their faith.

Addressing Spiritual Questions

Children and young adults often have questions about faith and spirituality. Addressing these questions openly and thoughtfully is crucial for nurturing a strong spiritual foundation.

Open Dialogue: Foster an environment where questions about faith are welcomed and discussed. Be honest about your own faith journey and share how you've navigated doubts and questions.

Seeking Answers Together: Explore questions together through Bible study, discussions with faith leaders, and reading faith-based literature. Show that seeking understanding is a valuable part of the faith journey.

Respecting Individual Journeys: Respect that each child's spiritual journey is unique. Provide guidance and support while allowing them the space to explore and develop their faith independently.

Parenting with Purpose:
Character Development Through Faith

Instilling Moral Values

Instilling moral values rooted in biblical principles is fundamental for guiding children in making ethical and compassionate decisions. Micah 6:8 (NIV) reminds us, "He has shown you, O mortal, what is good. And what does the Lord require of you? To act justly and to love mercy and to walk humbly with your God."

Teaching Right and Wrong: Use biblical teachings to explain concepts of right and wrong. Discuss stories and parables that illustrate moral lessons and ethical behavior.

Modeling Integrity: Demonstrate integrity and honesty in your actions. Show how living according to God's principles leads to a fulfilling and meaningful life.

Encouraging Compassion: Encourage acts of kindness, generosity, and compassion. Provide opportunities for children to serve others and make a positive impact in their community.

Parenting with Purpose:
Character Development Through Faith

Supporting Spiritual Growth Through Challenges

Supporting spiritual growth through challenges helps children and young adults develop resilience and trust in God's plan. Romans 5:3-4 (NIV) states, "Not only so, but we also glory in our sufferings, because we know that suffering produces perseverance; perseverance, character; and character, hope."

Facing Adversity: Discuss how faith can provide strength and comfort during difficult times. Share stories of biblical figures who faced challenges and relied on God for support.

Encouraging Perseverance: Encourage perseverance and faithfulness, even when faced with obstacles. Remind children of God's promises and the hope found in Him.

Finding Meaning in Struggles: Help children find meaning and growth in their struggles. Discuss how challenges can strengthen their faith and deepen their relationship with God.

Parenting with Purpose:
Character Development Through Faith

Creating a Faith-Filled Home Environment

Creating a faith-filled home environment nurtures a sense of peace, love, and spiritual growth. Joshua 24:15 (NIV) declares, "But as for me and my household, we will serve the Lord."

Spiritual Traditions: Establish spiritual traditions that reinforce faith, such as family prayers, scripture readings, and celebrating religious holidays.

Positive Atmosphere: Foster a positive and loving atmosphere where faith is integrated into daily life. Encourage gratitude, forgiveness, and mutual respect.

Faith-Based Resources: Provide access to faith-based resources, including books, music, and media. Surround children with materials that inspire and strengthen their faith.

Conclusion

Nurturing faith and building a strong spiritual foundation in children and young adults is a vital aspect of parenting. By leading by example, encouraging personal faith practices, addressing spiritual questions, instilling moral values, supporting spiritual growth through challenges, and creating a faith-filled home environment, we guide our children in developing a deep, abiding faith. Proverbs 22:6 (NIV) reminds us of the enduring impact of a strong spiritual foundation. As we nurture our children's faith, we equip them to navigate life with confidence, integrity, and a profound sense of purpose rooted in their relationship with God.

Chapter 15
The Journey of Parenthood

Reflecting on Lessons Learned and Embracing the Future

The journey of parenthood is a profound and transformative experience, filled with joys, challenges, and invaluable lessons. As we reflect on the lessons learned and embrace the future, we draw on the wisdom of Proverbs 3:5-6 (NIV): "Trust in the Lord with all your heart and lean not on your own understanding; in all your ways submit to him, and he will make your paths straight."

Reflecting on Lessons Learned

Reflecting on the lessons learned throughout the parenting journey allows us to grow and find deeper meaning in our experiences.

Embracing Imperfection: Understand that no parent is perfect, and mistakes are part of the journey. Use these moments as opportunities for growth and learning.

Valuing the Present: Cherish the present moments with your children. Recognize the fleeting nature of time and make the most of each stage of their development.

Parenting with Purpose: Character Development Through Faith

Learning from Challenges: Reflect on the challenges faced and the resilience developed. Acknowledge the ways in which overcoming difficulties has strengthened your family.

Embracing the Future with Hope

As our children grow and embark on their own paths, we embrace the future with hope, trusting in God's plan for their lives.

Supporting Independence: Encourage your children's independence and support their individual journeys. Trust in the foundation you've provided and their ability to navigate the world.

Staying Connected: Maintain a strong, loving connection with your children as they enter adulthood. Continue to offer guidance, support, and unconditional love.

Trusting God's Plan: Place your trust in God's plan for your children and your family. Remember Jeremiah 29:11 (NIV): "For I know the plans I have for you," declares the Lord, "plans to prosper you and not to harm you, plans to give you hope and a future."

Celebrating Milestones

Celebrating milestones and achievements allows us to recognize the progress and growth of our children and family.

Graduations and Achievements: Celebrate educational milestones, achievements, and personal successes. Acknowledge the hard work and dedication of your children.

Life Transitions: Embrace significant life transitions, such as entering the workforce, getting married, or becoming parents themselves. Support your children in these new chapters of their lives.

Family Traditions: Continue family traditions that celebrate milestones and create lasting memories. These traditions reinforce a sense of belonging and continuity.

Fostering Lifelong Learning and Growth

Encourage lifelong learning and growth for both yourself and your children. Proverbs 1:5 (NIV) states, "Let the wise listen and add to their learning, and let the discerning get guidance."

Continuous Improvement: Strive for continuous improvement in your parenting and personal development. Seek out resources, support, and opportunities for growth.

Encouraging Curiosity: Foster a love of learning and curiosity in your children. Encourage them to explore new interests, pursue knowledge, and develop new skills.

Modeling Lifelong Learning: Demonstrate the importance of lifelong learning by pursuing your own education and personal growth. Share your experiences and insights with your children.

Conclusion
The Legacy of Faith and Love

The legacy of faith and love we leave for our children is the most enduring and impactful gift we can offer. As we conclude this journey of parenthood, we are reminded of 1 Corinthians 13:13 (NIV): "And now these three remain: faith, hope and love. But the greatest of these is love."

Faith: Nurture a strong, abiding faith that guides your children's lives and decisions. Trust in God's plan and His presence in your family's journey.

Hope: Instill a sense of hope and optimism in your children. Encourage them to look forward to the future with confidence and trust in God's promises.

Love: Above all, love unconditionally. Show your children the power of love through your actions, words, and unwavering support.

Parenting with Purpose:
Character Development Through Faith

Final Thoughts

Parenthood is a sacred and transformative journey that shapes the lives of both parents and children. By reflecting on lessons learned, embracing the future with hope, celebrating milestones, fostering lifelong learning, and leaving a legacy of faith and love, we fulfill our God-given role as parents. Proverbs 3:5-6 (NIV) encourages us to trust in the Lord and lean on His guidance as we navigate the complexities and joys of parenthood. With faith, hope, and love as our foundation, we can confidently embrace the journey ahead, knowing that we are raising our children in accordance with God's will and purpose.

www.ingramcontent.com/pod-product-compliance
Lightning Source LLC
Chambersburg PA
CBHW070949180426
43194CB00041B/1843